Down to the Quick

Nancy Scott

Plain View Press
P. O. 42255
Austin, TX 78704

plainviewpress.net
sbright1@austin.rr.com
1-512-440-7139

Copyright Nancy Scott, 2007.
All rights reserved.
ISBN: 978-1-891386-63-3
Library of Congress Control Number: 2006932943

Acknowledgments

The following publications published poems included in this collection. *Exit 13*: Lake Oxbow, WI, Traveling South by Train through Northern Florida in the 1950's, Tuscany; *Flint Hills Review:* Boston's Great Molasses Flood, 1919; *Jewish Women's Literary Annual:* Wedding Day, Burlingame, CA, Egg Market; *Journal of New Jersey Poets:* Whatever Happened to Ten Young Black Men from New Jersey, When Balfour Calls, Why I Never Want to Be a Trenton Landlord; *Kelsey Review:* Meeting Princess Grace, The Whistler; *The Ledge*: Hot Pepper Salsa; *The Lullwater Review:* Sarah at Fifteen; *Mudfish:* Miami's First POW Home from Korea, 1953; *Out of Line:* Sometimes What We Miss, Child's Play, circa 1944, Herman Sharp (1899-1918), Lake Carnegie, Late Afternoon, The Haunting of Alejandro, Lost Boy of Sudan, Cousin Leon and the Playboy Bunny; *Papyrus:* Adoption Match Party, Eighteenth Birthday; *Rattapallax:* My Trouble, Not Yours; *Riverrun:* The Sweater Poem; *Slant:* The Good Witch, The Point, Chicago, 1959, Dim Sum, San Francisco, 118 Maida Vale, London; *Slipstream:* The Ship Builder; *Struggle*: Life After Welfare Reform; *U.S.1 Worksheets:* Animal Planters, Down to the Quick, The Shearling; *Witness:* The Rug Shop

Cover Art: *The Closing Night Party*, de Young Museum, San Francisco, public art project, © Kurt Stoeckel and Martin Whitney, 2006.

Contents

Down to the Quick

My Trouble, Not Yours	9
Late October	10
Lake Oxbow, WI	11
Cousin Leon and the Playboy Bunny	12
Summer	13
Baptist Graduate House, Chicago, 1959	14
My Tutor, Chicago, 1959	15
The Good Humor Man, 1960	16
Wedding in Fargo, 1960	17
Child's Play, circa 1944	18
Dinner at *Louie's Grill*	20
Down to the Quick	22
Camera Angle	23
Egg Market	24
The Point, Chicago, 1959	25
Animal Planters	26
The Good Witch	27
Sarah at Fifteen	28
Easter Week	30
Hot Pepper Salsa	32
The Sweater Poem, 1960	33
Artichokes, Big Sur	34
Wedding Day, Burlingame, CA	35
Dim Sum, San Francisco	37

Boot Camp

Sometimes What We Miss	41
Lake Carnegie, Late Afternoon	42
The Haunting of Alejandro	43
In Absecon	45
Whatever Happened To Ten Young Black Men from New Jersey	46
The Shearling	49

When Balfour Calls · 50
Meeting Princess Grace · 51
The White Suit · 52
The Apartment Inspection · 54
Life After Welfare Reform · 55
Fish Bones · 57
Chester's Screaming · 58
Lily · 59
Why I Never Want to Be a Trenton Landlord · 60
Adoption Match Party · 62
Eighteenth Birthday · 64
Dandelion, a foster child · 65
Lone Black Juror Votes Not to Acquit · 66
The Sixth Child · 67
314 Spruce Street · 68
Boot Camp, Graduation Day · 69

Feeling My Way With A Fork

The Ship Builder · 73
Early December · 74
The Whistler · 75
If I am fit to kill, am I fit to live? · 76
Satellite Dish, Levittown, PA · 77
Delicate Balance · 78
Miami's First POW Home from Korea, 1953 · 80
Herman Sharp (1899-1918) · 81
Boston's Great Molasses Flood, 1919 · 82
The Bear · 83
Saving Lives · 84
Lost Boy of Sudan · 85
Lost Boy of Sudan, part 2 · 86
You Know What I'm Sayin' · 87
Traveling South by Train through Northern
    Florida in the 1950's · 89
The Breaking Yard, Alang, India · 90
Curacao, 1968, Before the Insurrection · 92
English Summer, Idmiston, Wiltshire · 93

118 Maida Vale, London	94
The Rug Shop	95
The Italian Photo	96
Tuscany	97
Cherry Cheesecake	99
Lark Sparrow	100
About the Author	103

Down to the Quick

A wind that is time alternates with a wind that is place, and God remains down here like a man who thinks he's forgotten something, and will stick around until he remembers.
                                        Yehudi Amichai

My Trouble, Not Yours

It's not about color,
taut strings of silence
or your turbulent heart
when night suckles demons.

It's a raindrop riff
as wind switches voices,
bodies glistened with sweat,
you, sleek as a panther,
stalking my mind.

Late October

It's rained for hours.
An unmistakable smell of decay
rises from dead leaves piled at the curb.
My grandsons are wrestling
on the living room floor.
Perhaps the one who's pinned
hopes I'll intervene.
Soon they'll climb into their bunk beds
and trade insults until they drop off to sleep.

I'm watching the nightly news:
in Trenton, a young girl waiting
to cross the street has been killed
by a stray bullet. A man hugs
the distraught mother.
Outside our window, the trees, stripped
of leaves, stand like barbed sentries.
No moon, just an icy glaze forming
on wet pavement.

Lake Oxbow, WI

My brother and I inherited seven acres.
Richard wants to sell it, needs cash.
Says he doesn't remember the last summer
we spent at the lake. He was eight.
I was sixteen in love with Peter.

I remember how we dove off the raft,
chilled water tugging our feet, stinging
our sunburned shoulders, then hiking miles
to the general store for magazines and soda pop.

I remember long evenings – card games,
Monopoly, jig-saw puzzles – waiting for
parents to go to bed. Sneaking out
under a fury of stars, we'd row to a secluded cove,
oars softly turning the water.
Peter's blond hair shimmering, tentative kisses,
promises rippling against the shore.

I remember land unsevered, before backhoe,
buzzsaw, swirl of motor oil on the water;
I remember March 28th, the day Peter died
asleep at the wheel, his Chevy ramming a pole.

I never went back to Oxbow again.
My brother says lake frontage is worth a bundle.

Cousin Leon
and the Playboy Bunny

– for L.L., 1945-1971

They warned him
she belonged to the Cuban.
The second time
they busted his mouth
and fractured three ribs.
He shipped out to Nam.
She came to him at night
during long, waking patrols,
her lips wet and luscious.
By day, bare shoulders
cloaked in rough cloth,
she tracked at his side,
kept on through minefields
and enemy fire.

When he returned
he found her serving cocktails
in North Miami Beach.
"Babe, I've missed you,"
he said, his voice husky.
Cool fingers deftly grazed
his cheek. She shed
her satin ears and cotton tail
and went with him.
In late March, his body
floated up
in an isolated cove,
a single bullet
to the back of his head.

Summer

An elderly woman
sits alone on a bench at the bus stop,
waiting for something, maybe the 609,
maybe her dead husband.
We all wait for the sun.

Incessant rain has sent small stones
and dirt clods tumbling down
the embankment in my backyard.
I can feel my house inch
closer to extinction.

Last summer, people complained
about drought, stunted corn,
impassable spots in the river.
Dry needles flared across acres.
We longed to hear rain beating on the roof.

Everywhere there is excess.
No hope to change the progress of the wind.
It will blow away the clouds or won't.
I am stitching squares
for my granddaughter's quilt.

Baptist Graduate House, Chicago, 1959

The summer I met Calvin
he'd just finished med school.
By chance, we lived
in a converted mansion
where we shared communal chores.

I'd watch his dark strong hands
mincing onions, folding napkins,
stirring pots of thick tomato sauce,
imagining how those hands
would save a life.

You'll be damaged goods,
my mother had warned,
if you're seen with colored men.

Late one afternoon,
I wandered stifling rooms.
I hated Chicago's dog days, hated
reading 16th C. texts I didn't understand.

As if by silent bidding, Calvin appeared,
his arms, dark wings around me,
his cheek against my sun-bleached hair
in the familiar way of lovers.

I've wanted to do this all summer, he said.
His heart-strength in the seamless air
stanched the flow of self-pity.

To summer's end, we never spoke
about that moment, but prepared
the evening meal in the ordinary way.
Outside these walls, any possibility
would be too dear.

My Tutor, Chicago, 1959

Grey tomb building
quiet campus study
narrow leaded windows
books and more books
colorful spines
warming stone walls.
I sat beside you
at a polished oak table.
You described form and essence
of poetic thought, legacy
of Elizabethan poets made
more intriguing by your energy.
Your yellow pencil
tapping stresses.

You took me to hear
Martin Luther King.
South of Evansville, you said,
They called you *boy*.
One Sunday afternoon,
cold, biting wind,
we drove to a secluded spot
along the lake. We spoke
about free will and existential things
of forging friendships.
The moment marred:
raps insistent on my window
the police asking
Miss, are you all right?

The Good Humor Man, 1960

Dorothy's dating the Good Humor Man
but we're gorging ourselves
on fudge ripple sundaes
smothered in gobs of whipped cream.
Sometimes I crave the real stuff, she says,
not stored in his truck for months.

She complains he brings her
torpedo pops or almond crunch bars
when what she wants is red roses.
(or maybe it's because
he's got six toes on each foot)

He's part of an illustrious history, she says.
Ice cream has been around 3000 years.
Is that so? I wonder where this is going.
Marco Polo discovered it in China.
Montezuma poured hot chocolate over it.
Dolley Madison was famous for
her frozen pink cream.

I'm licking my spoon as she prattles on.
When great grandma was a child,
the Hokey Pokey Man stood on a corner
yelling, *a penny for a lump*, instead of
jingling those crazy bells
and tooling around in a truck.

Why persist with the history lesson?
By now, the rest of her sundae is soup.
It's the toes.
Yes. It's got to be those twelve toes.

Wedding in Fargo, 1960

I was one of six bridesmaids
in a canary cap-sleeved dress
and dyed-to-match satin pumps
which I left behind
on the way out of town
during a freak summer blizzard.

The bride, a petite Swedish blonde,
my roommate from college, who'd said,
I've come East to study Ibsen,
translated – *I'm at Chicago to find a husband*.

We'd shared an apartment on Hyde Park Blvd.
Dorothy discarded two guys named Ted,
one with six toes, the other a Texas preacher,
hooked up with Tom, a wired artist,
after he'd painted a life-sized lion
snarling on our living room wall, with oils,
the kind that takes four coats to cover,
like goose grease spatters
when our holiday bird blew up in the stove.

The wedding was acres of tulle, champagne,
and tomato aspic, the groom in tails, his beard
untamed. I prayed for the marriage.
Tom could swallow Dorothy with his roar,
she had a way of dissolving,
leaving fisted words
that could make snow-laden corn stand tall.

Child's Play, circa 1944

Tommy let me look at the snakeskins
in his cigar box. I told him where
my dad kept his shotgun and shells.
He begged me to show him
but I never did.

When Tommy got into one of his moods,
he'd straddle the crotch of the maple,
set his bow and arrow and....ZING
Purdy's cat scooted yeowing up the street.

Or, on the way home from school,
he'd catch me at the railroad crossing.
Grab a long stick from the bushes,
taunt me as I backed closer
and closer to the hot third rail.

Go home, I'd call out, from my perch
on the jungle gym, *I don't want to play.*
Tommy threw rocks, swung his baseball bat
at my dangling feet.
I'll tell my daddy, voice shrieking.
He'll blast you away with his shotgun.

That summer kids on the block played at war,
lobbed sand-bag socks, water balloons
from the safety of Purdy's brick wall.

The next day we'd start again, the boys
fighting over who got to be 'good guys',
who got to be 'Nazis'. The girls
mostly waved flags or made bandages.

We never let Tommy join in.
He'd hunch on the curb and watch, whipping
his stick in the air. Dreamed about shooting
a real gun, real bullets. Killed more enemy
in his mind than those lying dead on the grass
if the war only lasted ten more years.

Dinner at *Louie's Grill*

My father and I smile over sweaty dishes.
I pick a green olive from the relish tray, suck out

a pimento, occupy my mouth so I can't speak.
Six ice-bedded shrimp, tails hooked

in choppy red sauce, untouched in fluted glass.
The shrimp have black strings along their spines.

Three-pronged fork poised, my father asks,
Do you want me to go back to your mother?

I stab a shrimp, examine it, tear bread hunks
into small pieces, scattering crumbs.

*

My mother hot for prey, yanks off my quilt,
leans over me, her breath reeking of bourbon,

*Your father doesn't love you. You're a fool.
He only thinks about himself.*

She curses the man whose Lincoln was parked
in the redheaded whore's driveway.

*

My father never mentions the redhead, devours
the shrimp, oblivious of the black veins.

I want my father to own up to the affair
so I can forgive him.

Are you finished? The waiter head snaps
back, forth. My *daughter doesn't like shrimp,*

my father says. Eyes hungry for an answer,
he leans across the white expanse of cloth.

You left me behind strangles in my throat.
I say, *Whatever will make you happy.*

Down to the Quick

At the funeral
well-meaning relatives
try to convince me
to take a last look at my father
I knew the moment
he'd died miles away
on the sidewalk
another middle-aged man
having a coronary
it felt like a stab wound
that wouldn't stop bleeding
like the dream
I have over & over
we sit at a table
in the dimly-lit room
no one else is around
I'm biting my nails
down to the quick
he's peering over
the top of his bifocals
forget me he says
jo & her kids need me now
I want to scream
jo's a drunk & those girls
have a father
it won't ever happen
you're dead
and you're mine.

Camera Angle

from a photo taken on the 1ˢᵗ Street jetty, Miami Beach

Someone took the black and white of the four
barefoot on the jetty. Maybe the blonde, thrusting
her tits, bright red lips slightly parted, tapped

the arm of an old man wearing a pink flamingo
shirt and handed him the camera. As he caught
her likeness, his balls probably started tingling.

The guy in khakis has an arm around the brunette,
so the other guy sitting alone, stomach bloated,
eyes sunken like he'd been in a prisoner-of-war camp,

must be the blonde's boyfriend. How did those two
hook up? Maybe he'd just gotten home from a war
and the blonde figured he must be horny so she called

and asked him out; he thought, why not? Maybe
he'd been having nightmares, waking in a sweat,
the bamboo cage too small for him to stand up in

and he couldn't sit because the ground was covered
with excrement. Now he can't remember the blonde's
name, she feels like another dream he isn't ready for yet.

He stares at the old man clicking the shutter, then
watches the blonde go over, take the camera and brush
her tits against the flamingos on the old man's shirt.

Egg Market

Medium, extra-large, jumbo,
high omega, vegetarian, free-range.

Ivy League newspaper ad reads:
Wanted: Jewish eggs, $10,000 – $50,000 paid.
Donor must have minimum 1500 SAT scores,
22 to 28 years, 5'5" to 5'9",
at least, one Jewish grandparent.

Scores verified, affidavit of lineage required.
Highest rates: four Jewish grandparents

Sounds pricey, though Beluga or Fabergé
might fetch heftier sums.

I meet some requirements, including
optimal number of grandparents.

I wonder how much I could get.
Pity, I have no eggs left.

The Point, Chicago, 1959

At the Point this summer afternoon,
the sun furious with heat, our beach towels

sprawl along the limestone blocks
descending like steps into Lake Michigan.

You're absorbed in some Russian abstract.
I step gingerly into the lake, chilled water

curling around my ankles like a serpent.
A coal barge silhouetted on the horizon.

Behind us a lush meadow, where
last spring, I'd taken my Girl Scout troop,

black girls from the South Side, crossing
the few blocks from their homes,

climbing invisible fences for the first time
to play softball and run relay races.

We'd unpacked hot dogs and potatoes to roast,
discovered we'd forgotten charcoal for the grill.

The girls ducked behind me as two policemen
approached. I expected some humiliation.

Instead they asked if we needed anything,
came back later carrying a bag of charcoal.

You look up and smile, distracted by a speed boat
churning up the water, ask if I want suntan oil

rubbed on my back. We're both as white as gulls
that lift and settle freely on the limestone.

Animal Planters

It was freezing today at the flea market,
not much for sale, not a cent on me.
With a checkbook, it's never too cold to haggle.
I bought an elephant, right foot nudging a blue ball,
ears flared, trunk curled upward in triumph.

When it comes to animal planters, I've no willpower.
My shelves are lined: three kittens in shoe,
grinning bear on log, cocker spaniel under mailbox.
Not to mention koala hugging tree,
buck-toothed rabbit or kangaroo,
ponies, swans, dogs, donkeys, ducks,
two deer, fawn and doe intertwined,
green stallion flying, red fox and a maroon goose
with a polka-dot kerchief.

Last week as I lingered at his table, a seller asks,
Aren't you the lady who bought a wood duck?
Oh, you remembered, I answer to save time
from haggling over two planter/bookends,
magnificent rams' heads, though
I couldn't say which of my wood ducks he meant.

I've found them from Montreal to San Francisco,
in Boston's antique shoppes, dusty barns in Ohio.
I still grieve for the overpriced cockatoo in Canton,
slightly chipped panther left behind.
Thousands wait to be saved from the dumpster.
It's only a matter of shelf space and stamina.
I can't stop. I've become the SPCA for animal planters.

The Good Witch

My daughter brings home a wren
with a broken wing. She is crying.
She asks me to fix it.
I'm good at fixing things –
clogged drains, flat tires, a lopsided cake.
I don't know how to fix
a broken wing.

When I was young, I had a white canary.
I forgot to feed it or give it water
or change the newspaper in its cage.
I was busy being a child.
One day I found it curled up
under its feeding dish, stiff
as the fake birds on our Christmas tree.
I threw it out my bedroom window,
hoping it would fly.
I do not tell my daughter this.
She's still crying. Her wren
is shivering on the countertop.

An old, bent woman lives on the block.
She cares for sick animals
and sings to them in Polish.
The children make fun of her.
They call her *witch*, say animals
don't know Polish.
She grows lush tomatoes and string beans.
Sunflowers line her fence.
She lets rabbits eat her lettuce.

We put the wren in a shoe box
and my daughter bravely goes to find her.

Sarah at Fifteen

had long, thick hair, the kind you sell
to the wigmaker for a fortune,
but she cuts it to inches, sprays and spritzes it
until it has the texture of black meringue.

I watch as she threads a dozen gold hoops
through the holes in her ears.
Do you plan to pierce your tongue?
That's gross, she says.
A nose ring? No way.
Your eyebrow? She shakes her head.

Two days later, she rolls up her sleeve
shows me a Chinese symbol tattooed on her left upper arm.
It's okay, she assures me, Stephie and me found
this really cool shop and the guy who did it uses clean needles.

The note says she hasn't been going to class, spends
most of her time in the parking lot smoking.
What do you plan to do with your life?
I'm going to college.
But you don't go to class.
She hugs me in a halo of musk,
I will when I get to college.

She takes up with George who gives her stolen CD's
and a shearling I can't afford.
Return them, I insist.
Don't you love it, she oozes, caressing the jacket.

She flounces into the kitchen.
George is history, she snarls, rips the tab off a coke.
Then he's at the door with those wary timber wolf eyes.
My gran threw me out. Before I can blink,
my daughter grabs up his backpack, invites him in.

I underestimate George. It takes a court order
to uproot him. Bribe of new Nikes and rap concert tickets
to get Sarah back into class.
Oh, sweet victory – until I catch them
in the kitchen cooking spaghetti, their hair
streaked with purple, grinning as wide as the moon.

Easter Week

We meet over shopping carts
dodging lilies, tulips, hyacinths.
We live only three miles apart,

haven't spoken for years.
Then we're drinking coffee
catching up on everything

from impending retirement
to Pre-Raphaelites.
I'm waiting for the zinger.

I hear from Joe every few years,
Kate says. *He's in the Southwest.*
Albuquerque, I say.

Easter week, twenty years ago
Joe and I had an affair.
Hell, Kate was married to someone

else, but she never forgave us.
Even now, she can't help herself.
Joe's story always gets grimmer.

He was stealing big time, she says.
Had to leave town.
She'd look ten years younger

if she'd get her eyelids done.
Although she swears it isn't so,
I'm sure she dyes her hair.

Joe married a bitch, she says.
I wouldn't know, I say,
looking at my watch.

My coffee cup is empty.
I have tulips in the car,
wilting.

Hot Pepper Salsa

Trucker kills Self, <u>The Times</u>, Trenton, 2000

Can we find solace in hot pepper salsa?

Sarah fills the basket with cashews, cream crackers,
pears, chocolate truffles and terra blue chips
to scoop up the salsa.
For his family, she says, *the guys all pitched in.*

How many times did he threaten to do it?
Stop kidding, we said.
How many times did we hear it?
Yeah, yeah. Then we passed round the beer,
kicked back and wide-screened the Jets.

He was a really nice guy, Sarah says
as she adds a tin of buttery shortbread.

He wanted his ex-girlfriend there when he did it.
Just her.
Instead he found himself surrounded by
squad cars and cops.
He put the gun to his chest and fired once.
Just once.

Do you think it's enough? Sarah asks
shrink-wrapping the basket, tying
red ribbon so neatly.

How much will it take to ease the *ifs*
that sear the tongue like hot pepper salsa?

The Sweater Poem, 1960

We flirted in a whirlwind
of summer courses
at Stanford.
Rafael's father was president
of the largest bank in Chile.
Rafael had raven's hair
and an arrogant way
of locking his hip.
One cool July night
we closed a Los Altos bar,
leaned against
the hood of his Porsche
in the parking lot,
smoking Luckies.
Quarreling.
I was shivering
in a skimpy black sheath.
Rafael rifled his trunk
for a dark grey
cable-stitched, crew neck
cashmere sweater.
I suppose if your father's a big-shot,
you don't miss
an expensive sweater.
Years later,
I can't remember why
I've kept it.

Artichokes, Big Sur

She's never driven on the coastal highway,
never seen surf crash against the rocks
or bait and tackle shops, small craft
nesting on the shore.

He pulls the jeep up to a roadside stand.
Artichokes – five for a dollar.
He buys a plastic bag full.

She's in college, knows about Plath,
Tolstoy, and the Peloponnesian Wars.
She's never tasted an artichoke.

What part do you eat? she asks.
You pull off the leaves, he says, *and dip
the ends in melted butter.*

She's a strict Catholic. Her family
came from Aguascalientes.
Her father drives a Mercedes.

You scrape the ends with your teeth.
He winks at her. *You'll like them.*
She thinks she loves this young man,

but he's divorced and has a daughter.
Her father refuses to meet him.
I don't know, she says, tossing
the plastic bag into the back seat.

Wedding Day
Burlingame, CA

The groom waits in a white gazebo perched
on a promontory overlooking the golf course.

Wind and fog swoop down in great drafts.
The temperature hovers in the 50's.

Two flower girls shriek against the wind
and refuse to walk down the aisle.

The bride arrives in a glass pumpkin coach
drawn by a team of black horses.

The bride's father struggles to untwirl
his daughter's veil which threatens to take flight.

The sound system sputters music from *Titanic*.
The microphone hisses. A sudden gust separates

the priest from his sheaf of vows and prayers.
He calls the groom by the wrong name.

I am the mother of the groom, layered in
everything warm I'd brought from New Jersey.

My ex-husband is seated next to me. Haven't seen
him in seven years. He's blowing his nose.

It's the wind, he says, although he might be
showing some emotion I don't recognize.

The bride's family is Mexican. The priest delivers
prayers in Spanish, vows in English.

The groom doesn't speak Spanish. The priest
asks everyone to hug the person next to them.

I'd rather sink my teeth into my ex-husband's neck,
but I don't want to create a scene. We embrace.

The priest drapes white rosary beads and a cross
around the bride and groom. Ghosts

of my Jewish ancestors howl around
flower displays chained to the gazebo.

Later there are Mariachis and lots of tequila.
The bride's brother croons songs in Spanish.

The groom dances with Mexican ladies
who stick $100 bills behind his ear, in his belt.

The chicken dinner is cold. My ex-husband looks
at his watch. *I'm a senior citizen*, he says.

I need my sleep. He gets up and leaves.
The bride's father staggers from table to table.

The bride is yelling at the groom, something
about the wine. Everyone else is doing the salsa.

Dim Sum, San Francisco

The tray is spinning pork dumplings,
stuffed mushrooms, marinated eggplant,
and something fried and leggy.
It's seven years since I've seen
my ex-husband who's sitting
across the table, asking if I need a fork.
Stacked bamboo baskets keep coming.
We shoo away waiters, search for
safe conversation. I ask about his recent trip
to Salisbury where one summer
we rented a half-timbered vicarage.
Talk drifts to the Saturday market.
*I've never seen so many shoppers
with disfigurements*, my ex says,
as he scoops up mango pudding.
I remember browsing that market,
selecting tart apples and figs, fresh bread
and bangers. Among rusty tools and smell
of tanned leather, would I now find
cleft lips, club feet and flippers?
Could it be Porton? I say. Maybe
contaminated soil, genetic mutations
from the chemical warfare plant
hidden a few kilometers away.
*George Pelly worked at Porton
for a few years*, my ex says.
*Now he's assigned to The Hague
as a terrorism expert.*
The summer I was in Salisbury,
George was a captain in the British Army.
We were wildly attracted.
Sounds perfect for George, I say, blandly.
Straight-limbed, fearless, he'd defused
bombs in Belfast, shot smugglers' camels

in the mountains of Yemen.
But I wasn't up for adventure
and stayed with the man
who's asking the waiter
to pack up the leftover Dim Sum.

Boot Camp

the fiercest wind comes forth now from inside a young girl's hand
Yehudi Amichai

Sometimes What We Miss

When she heard the child cry out,
her right arm jerked to a grotesque angle,
fingers splayed and froze.
She dragged her twisted right leg,
foot curled inward, as she limped
across the floor.

From its crib, the child reached out perfect arms,
kicked its bare feet against the bars,
insistent like a ragged shutter
on a windy night.

With her left hand, she squeezed rigid
fingers into a fist, bent her shoulders
and gently scooped the child with her forearms.
Gurgling, the child nuzzled against her neck.

She crooned a lullaby of lemon trees
and goat bells tinkling,
the music of laughter
of shoes dancing, hands clapping
to the beat of the tarantula.

In this way Rosalita taught the child
how to make its body sing.

Lake Carnegie, Late Afternoon

Orange sky
slips below the tree line.
College oarsmen, stroke by stroke,
slice ever-graying water.

On the road, arms awhirl,
a legless man, wheelchair-bound,
placard round his neck
– *I'm a homeless Vet.*

All race against the fading light,
resolute on course.
One outwitting midnight's chill,
others to the boathouse.

The Haunting of Alejandro

There was a brown-eyed girl behind the counter
pouring coffee, her smile making you believe
something good could happen.

She quit last week, they said when you went back.

You stalked her ghost for months,
like you'd read your mother's shadow
in every stranger passing
where your mother left you, nine years old.
Dealing your way through shrill streets,
razor-thin highs.

      *

When you'd given up, she appeared,
the brown-eyed girl.
An ordinary intersection, amber light
holding her back, she turned and smiled.

      *

Your body, seething like tinder ready to flare.
Why did you risk it?
This girl you seduced with such tenderness.

Did you tell her how you'd felt your body change?
Something gone wrong, long before you turned
twenty, fourteen maybe. The itchiness inside.

Did you make her understand
when she took you into her, what flowed from you
could have killed her?

        continued

*

Today you cradle your squawking son, rosy with life.
As you kiss him quiet, his body molds to the curve
of your arm, eyelids twitter and close.

You bargain with God to see the first molar, first haircut,
the wind at his back as he races after the ball.

*

This mother, this girl. What is she dreaming
each time
she puts your son to her breast?

When they lay you to ground, how will she tell it?

Can there be any other way than to gather your son
in her arms? *Milagro*, miracle.

In Absecon

A blond man gaunt with AIDS
teaches his dark infected foster child
a nursery rhyme.
Word by spout he becomes a teapot,
spout by arm she mimics him.

Dying man, dying child.

Tulips whirl on her pinafore,
as he lifts her to his bone-thin hip.
More, she cries.
He shakes his head.
Tomorrow. No more today.

Whatever Happened To Ten Young Black Men from New Jersey

Woody sat on our sofa, gobbled buttered popcorn,
watched MTV and said he wanted to join
the Army after high school. Home on leave,
he used a two-by-four to fend off
his doped-up cousin. Cops shot Woody in the head.

And then there were nine

After Terry got a college football scholarship,
something went wrong. He argued
with his girlfriend, wrote a dozen letters,
including one to my daughter, took a stolen
revolver into the closet, and pulled the trigger.

And then there were eight

My daughter showed me pinkish stains
on the sidewalk where Reuben took
a random bullet in a driveby. Would have
bled to death if a passing nurse
hadn't plunged her hands into the wound.
An allergic reaction to medication killed him.

And then there were seven

It happened so fast in the parking lot
of the Merry-Go-Round Club. Tyrone
was opening the car door. The next minute
he was dead on the blacktop. The Club's
security officer was flirting with a teen
in a tight green dress.

And then there were six

Shamika had flawless fake nails, good legs,
long, straight hair that swished around
her shoulders. Dying from AIDS, she asked
to be buried as Bruce, how we knew her.

And then there were five

Balfour lived with us after his father threatened
to kill him with a machete. He's been in
and out of jail and rehab for the past ten years.
I pray he's all right but dread the next phone call.

And then there were four

He's got five years left of a ten-year stretch
for killing a drunk who hit him first.
Freshman in college, Bobby thought packing
a midnight special was cool. Now he wishes
he'd just walked away.

And then there were three

Lester found out he was HIV-positive
when he decided to give up cocaine.
T-cell count's 20 after years on the cocktail.
He spends hours waiting at the clinic
and going to funerals.

Now there are two

My son, Jimmy, coaches his daughter's soccer,
drives a customized Jeep, wonders if
he can cover the next car payment
because his new wife loves to charge things
she doesn't need.

continued

And he is the one

Lamont puts in a sixty-hour week driving
a truck, watches Sunday football with his brothers,
runs errands for his mom. He wants to marry
my daughter. She says he's nice but
he likes to be in charge.

The Shearling

Georgie's mom turned him out, a skinny five-year old,
to steal. The welfare check and what men paid her went
for angel dust. At first he lifted bread, cigarettes, gummy bears,
packs of franks. Shopkeepers looked away, knew his mom
and felt sorry for the kid. By fourteen, Georgie was out the door
faster than imagination, his girdle lined with CD's, Nike sneakers,
Polo cologne, anything he could load in an outsized backpack,
sell behind school bleachers. My daughter showed up wearing
a shearling jacket. A gift, she said – No matter, give it back. Anger
brought curiosity. How does he spirit a jacket off a chained rack?
Bypass security with those plastic censors attached? Georgie uses
his teeth, she explained. The shearling went back, only to appear
again and again, boxed at the front door, like a magician's rabbit
doomed to take another curtain call.

When Balfour Calls

he calls from a rehab center,
third one this year,
his voice echoing
like the underground oil drum
unearthed from our property,
black gunk oozing
through subterranean crevices.

What am I supposed to say?
If I set up an oil rig, I'd be rich
instead of those jackals
with (de)calibrated instruments,
deep in the pockets of the EPA.
Gee, I'm happy to hear from you,
whyinhellcan'tyougetyourlifetogether?

Silence.
I calculate. It's October.
This call will cost me sneakers,
sweats, a winter jacket,
boxed and mailed.
Are you mad at me? he asks.
No. I'm glad you're safe.

Meeting Princess Grace

She apologized for missing her appointment. Again.
This time she'd forgotten a history class or fired her husband's gun
through the kitchen wall.
It shattered the neighbor's mirror or maybe
something else, she couldn't remember.
Could she make it up to me?
Last year she offered me a glass of carrot juice and three figs
in a napkin because her husband was a Lebanese student,
but sometimes he worked at Cluck-U-Chicken
when the foreign drafts were late.
Today, she said, *I love you.* And I said, *This conversation is over.*
And she said, *Actually, I'm Princess Grace so I don't
need a rental subsidy.*

The White Suit

"I imagine blood creeping onto the front of his suit"
                    – fragment from an unknown source

No one can persuade him
to go for more surgery.
What if he died under the knife?
Who would protect his family
and baby coming?

Listening to words he doesn't
understand, Carlos clenches
and unclenches his fist
at the rental subsidy briefing
(because good things occasionally
happen even in the barrio).

He wears a white linen suit
white patent shoes
white string tie
and Panama hat with a yellow band.

The translator explains:
Carlos, his pregnant wife,
and child make their home
in a roach-infested welfare motel.
Headed home with a carton of milk
he took a gut full of lead
in a drug-involved crossfire
lucky to be alive
but his intestines are seeping.

I can see him dressed
in his Sunday clothes, sitting
in the shaded piazza sipping beer,
children chasing in the dusty road,
smell of jasmine in the air.

The Apartment Inspection

In the hall ceiling
a 2-foot square-cut, edged with molding.
Our eyes traveled to that molding
unprepared for what we saw: dark red stains
missed by the painter's brush.
Aja crossed herself and said, *I knew him.*

Life After Welfare Reform

The waiting room is jammed with chairs. Adults sit stone-faced,
clutch rumpled envelopes filled with birth certificates, social
security cards, alien registrations – their poverty passports.
They stare at outdated flyers, missed opportunities pinned to
dirty walls, in English and Spanish as if those who can't read will
somehow comprehend.

Children sit cross-legged on the floor, leaf through tattered
magazines, eyes on glossy ads for iMacs and muscle cars. The
entrance door opens and shuts, blurts drafts of cold air.
Chorus of coughs. A tired child whimpers.
Marisol shoves her shopping bags closer to her feet.

At welfare, Marisol signs in to be certified, fumbles with paystubs,
receipts, prays food stamps won't be cut any more. At WIC,
her six-month-old son, three-year-old twins are measured and
weighed, so she can claim formula, orange juice, Cheerios, peanut
butter, hardly enough to float her from paycheck to paycheck.

Summoned for eviction, she cowers outside the courtroom, listens
to words she can't understand. Two *abogados* arguing –
one for the landlord, one from Legal Aid.
When she gets to the front of the line for kids' winter coats,
the Salvation Army's got nothing left.

At the free clinic, Marisol crosses her fingers deep in her pockets,
waits for test results of her viral load, unwanted pregnancy,
hepatitis, x-rays for bruised ribs. The doctor reassures her with
proper care and medication, but she already owes last month's
rent, there's a shut-off notice from public service, and the twins
are sharing one winter coat.

continued

Loaded with bags of potluck donations, she takes three buses to get home where her older son cracks the back of roaches and keeps them in jars. After early Mass, she'll walk the children to daycare, check the clock in the corner *bodega*, then catch a taxi to get to work on time or an angry boss will find someone else to stuff envelopes for minimum wage.

Fish Bones

At the kitchen table,
the old woman gums fish bones
and chain-smokes Kents.

Not my mother, Shirlene says.
*Johnny left her for me to watch
'cause he didn't want her no more.*

The old woman waves an unlit cigarette.
Shirlene reaches into a pocket
retrieves a lighter, strikes a flame.

*Day before his cousin's wedding
in Georgia, they found Johnny dead
in a swimming pool*, Shirlene says.

She pours a cup of cold coffee
sets it within reach
of the old woman's gnarled hand.

*Johnny said he'd send money
but I guess
that ain't gonna happen now.*

Chester's Screaming

Man Stabs Elderly Neighbor, <u>The Home News</u>, *2001*

He said:
I know they're making snuff films in the downstairs apartment.
They've drilled holes in the ceiling so I can watch.
Every night a new girl. I got it all on tape.
How do you think they get rid of the bodies?
The other night I couldn't sleep. Too much screaming.
Called the landlord, but he said no one is making films.
Probably loud music or TV.
I tell him I heard voices screaming.
He'll talk to the tenants, he said.
But the screaming doesn't stop. Goes on during the day, too.
I can't stand it anymore. I went over to Minnie's house.
She fixed me lunch, hot soup and a tuna sandwich,
said, not to worry. If there's something going on,
the police will handle it. Not like they did with Mama.
I was only trying to help her. I didn't hit her.
Even she said I never laid a hand on her. Fucking police
pressed charges anyway, said Mama had bruises
on the side of her head and a broken nose that couldn't happen
except if I'd assaulted her. I did six months in county.
Lots of screaming there, too. Guards never let you forget
who's in charge. One guy liked to wail when he jacked off.
Hah. Pissed the guards. Me and him got into it over breakfast.
Said I stole his cap in the yard, then we're punching each other,
and next thing I know, they ship me off to Trenton State.
Nothing to it, two guys settling a score, but you know how it is.
I tell the shrink there, make the screaming go away. He gives
me pills, dumbs me up so I can have a little peace and quiet.
Now they're downstairs doing another poor girl.
Sometimes three, four of them taking turns.
I'll show you the tape. Just stop screaming at me.

Lily

The landlord calls her *the midget*.
I tell him it's rude, but he does it anyway
with some affection.

Barely four-feet-two-inches-tall,
Lily wants to move to a first floor apartment.
She's tired of lugging

her three young children of normal size
up a steep flight of stairs, along with
the groceries and folded laundry.

I often see her uptown
in the company of
handsome men over six-foot-tall.

Why I Never Want to Be a Trenton Landlord

Hooker in 1A calls at 2 a.m.
        complaining
Her apartment's a fucking freezer
        and the cops

Smashed in the front door
        raided 2B
Bullets flying broken glass

As he climbs out of bed, his wife's
        voice yammers
"Sell that pain in the…three years
        back taxes"

On the 20 min. ride down I-95
        he remembers
He forgot smoke alarm batteries
        again

Finds walls outside 2B peppered
        with bullets
Ceiling light filaments still screwed
        in the sockets

Yellow plastic strips criss-crossing
        the door
No screaming, no thumps, too cold

Even the stereos and wide-screen
        TV's are silent
Even the cockroaches have settled in

He stoops to pick up an orange
        soda can
Makes a mental note to contact
        the exterminator

Mail a letter to each tenant

> *Those who want to keep*
> *cockroaches as pets, need*
> *to live somewhere else*

Robe loosely tied, 1A flashes
        thigh
"Com'on in. Mama'll warm you up"

"Not now, baby." Bitch owes
        six months rent
Where'n hell is the damn padlock
        to the basement?

His throbbing head about to explode
        he steps over
used condoms, empty crack vials

Shoves the toolbox in the trunk
        no heat tonight
Some asshole stole the furnace

Adoption Match Party

Children's menu. Each child tagged with
colored ribbon, numbered like a daily special.

Sunday picnic in the park, fried chicken buckets,
lemonade. Children pet fat-bellied goats, swing
upside down from monkey bars.
Adults fan themselves in animated conversation.
A boom-box blares Boyz II Men's latest.
Teenage boys pass off the ball, attempt
the perfect layup.

Hey, someone calls his name.
Stomach muscles clench, reasons bubble
in his brain. He's thirteen, has asthma
and a temper which got him arrested.
A bald man picked him once, then returned him
like a Kani shirt that didn't fit.

"Tell me, young man, what you like to do?"
A stranger hides behind dark glasses, her voice
a shrill knife slicing through stale bread.
"Play basketball, ma'am."
Each time he answers that lame question,
he feels as if he's shrinking.
"Do you like school?"
"Yes, ma'am." He misses Spike, his cat.
It fell ten stories, splattered like a tomato.
"What's your best subject?"
He smiles at a foxy girl with braided hair.
"Math. I'm good at math, ma'am."

A familiar voice blasts *thank you all for coming*.
He sprints back to his jab of friends.
"You score?" they crowd around and ask.
He shrugs. "Naw," he says, then dribbles
the ball between his legs. Heads up.
His jump shot swishes through the net.

Eighteenth Birthday

Antoine learned how to be that extra child
in someone else's house,
wear hand-me-downs and skip meals,
the kid with the different last name.
If he made too much noise,
got in trouble at school,
or the foster payment came late,
his belongings got packed in a brown paper bag.
If a government car brought a stranger to ask,
How're you doing? bullshit like that,
his heart went ballistic, mouth kept silent.

One ordinary day, he heard words
like the slash of a box cutter,
Your dad's in jail, your mom's been sober,
we're taking you home.
This skinny twelve-year-old bolted,
ran barefoot down broken cement, shouted,
I'd rather be dead than go back there.

The day he turned eighteen
Antoine was put out of the shelter.
Baggy jeans,
immaculate Nikes,
hair twisted in dreads,
a stuffed backpack slung over his shoulder,
he stood at the curb with no place to go,
bouncing his head to a Walkman beat.

Dandelion, a foster child

This tousle-haired child weeps milky tears,
a dandelion severed too far from its roots.
Today she wheedles a hug, a balloon,
a ride on a mechanical horse.
She babbles and struts with 3-year-old guile
goading adults into loving her.

Where shadows dance on daisied walls
and matching chintz of a not-hers room,
she wakes in the dark without a whimper.
Rubs her eyes, a luminous blue,
then tiptoes through rooms
searching for her mother.

Tomorrow when she's thirteen,
she'll pack her diary, jeans and mascara,
lipstick her name on the mirror.
Stealing cash, she'll flee on the turn of night.
Thin silhouette at a random stop,
destination, an unknown city.

Wailing sirens will announce her arrival,
blue smoky hype hollow her eyes
in each frame of a digital camera.
From hunger to dust and the arms
of a stranger, final embrace
for this counterfeit child.

Kiss on the brow and bright gingham dress,
dandelion seeds feather up to the moon.

Lone Black Juror Votes Not to Acquit

Unarmed 16-year-old hit in the neck. His 14-year-old companion dies at the scene, gunshot wound to the head. Trenton, 1998

He'd been arrested before for stealing cars
        two years incarcerated; two months out

Steamy spring night/Dayglo sky erasing stars

He steals a Toyota, joyrides down Route 29
        3 a.m. swarm of cops
                in the War Memorial parking lot

Search lights blazing/helicopters buzzing
        hail of bullets/young girl dies

In this city where cops shoot at a fleeing car
        a 16-year-old is charged
                with manslaughter
        neighbors protest
                one more injustice
        the mayor shuffles
                the police department
and the jury deadlocks 11-1

The Sixth Child

She lived in a crib her first three years,
in a closet, often not fed.
Mom said she only had five.
When rescued, Annie could barely sit.

Today, with thin arms, she circles her food
and waits.
If she thinks you're not looking,
she squirrels away cheese, raisins, grapes,

deep in her pockets, under the rug,
between the cushions.
You give Annie what she wants,
and don't let on.

314 Spruce Street

No front door, just empty bottles,
styrofoam containers. Graffiti.
Buzzers in rows to ghost apartments.

Wisp of a boy in grey underwear
inches open the door to 3-C.
Can I speak with your mom?

Mama'll whip me if I wake her.
Tears stripe dirty cheeks.
She isn't here, is she?

Inside, blood-spattered walls,
thick crud, feast for roaches.
Maggots ransack open garbage.

In the cabinet just pancake mix.
Where's your mother?
The child stands mute on spindly legs.

An older boy appears, T-shirt says
God Loves Me. *Whatchu want?*
I need to talk to your mother.

He looks me over, calculating.
She gone to Auntie's
but she be back any minute.

Boot Camp, Graduation Day

The road to Wharton Tract runs straight

through thick Pine Barrens.

Low buildings hug blacktop, remote

within the State preserve.

Three platoons of adolescents.

Blue, yellow, red berets in lockstep march.

Yes sir, Sir, branded in memory.

Red platoon is graduating.

Six months ago, dope dealers, car thieves,

vandals. *Fuck this.*

Today, ribboned medals grace scrubbed necks.

Drill instructors, trained to tether rage, call out

nineteen names.

With parental pride, their voices quaver,

each hand grasped.

Clothes wilting, noonday glare,

relatives applaud.

They've come to gather sons once more,

sigh with expectation once more.

Feeling My Way With A Fork

And from time to time a new shipment of history arrives...
                                                    Yehudi Amichai

The Ship Builder

Perhaps by a quirk of hormonal imbalance
or a reckless moment of indecision,
she's neither a man nor a woman.

In our Victoria's Secret world
she's a nightmare – heavy brow,
ample breasts, and paw-like hands.

With these hands, she builds ship models
with popsicle sticks, tying
intricate knots, fully-rigged sails.

She explains it takes months to finish
a ship, paint and lacquer it, making sure
all the riggings are exactly right.

Suddenly her fingers are nimble and lithe.
It isn't a man or woman I see
but the mainsail taut in a steady wind.

Early December

This morning a thin glaze of snow
covered the ground. Gray sky
hung low over the treetops.
I met a friend for lunch.
She wanted to tell me her troubles,
same stories about her children,
and latest lover who'd left her.
Something new – her bull terrier
had eaten her silk panties and a box
of staples. I had no advice to give her.
I never liked the animal.
We ordered a mushroom pizza
from a waitress with black nail polish.
At the next table, a frazzled couple
tried to calm their wailing offspring.
It started to snow as we left the restaurant.
The forecasters were wrong.
I promised to call my friend later.
Maybe she'll find a trainer for her dog.
Driving home, I spotted two young boys,
mouths wide-open to the sky
stealing snowflakes.

The Whistler

A young man came to rent a room,
told me he had no job, no money.
How do you live? I asked.
I barter, he replied. I bet
you'd like a widescreen TV.
I shook my head.
Perhaps a new refrigerator?
I'd like the rent in cash.
A year's supply of frozen meat?
I'm a vegetarian.
He rapped his knuckles on the door,
I'll be back, he said,
and bounded down the front steps,
whistling.

If I am fit to kill, am I fit to live?

Night of the trucks.

On a deserted stretch north of Baghdad,
sixty seconds of pure instinct.

Smell of diesel fuel. The conflagration,
smoke roiling as one enemy truck explodes,

sparking others. Men on fire come running,
mortar round cuts a man in half.

At first, a sense of exhilaration, how easy
it is to pull the trigger, grateful

not to be charred and screaming.
If you hesitate, you won't survive.

In this macho culture, Did you see the way
I dropped that guy?

Memory is an amplifier.
Feeling neither brave nor joyous;

later, the worst hangover you can imagine.
Thousands of miles away, waking in a sweat,

especially when the wrong people die –
young girl with her nose blown off,

husband carrying his dead wife.
Scraps of flesh among the ashes.

Satellite Dish, Levittown, PA

Like a high-tech alien ear among acres of flaking paint,
        concrete gnomes, crab grass, rusting pick-ups,
relaying danger to its brain center, gray aluminum, low-slung ranch.

Twisted wrought-iron defends entry, roof shingles slope
        within inches of stockade fence, three narrow windows
make tough shot for semi-automatic drive-by or high-powered rifle
        from white birch cluster across the street, that seeks
mobster's rail-thin girlfriend in witness protection program,
        Colombian druglord chilling out at the expense of the CIA,
or maybe, an ordinary Joe just wants to watch sporting events
        on Sunday afternoons.

Remember Da Nang. Nightmares. Thumbs on his father's throat.
        He wanted to be a cop, needed discipline. Then
his buddy, a NYC cop, gunned down. In country all over again.

        Instead he became a state prison guard, recognized himself
in faces on the other side of the bars. Watching his back. Silence
at the end of the line. His truck license plates, easily traced.
Three daughters. Too damn much unobstructed space.

Delicate Balance

He can sit stone silent
like chiseled granite.
She wants to put a mirror
under his nose
to make sure he's breathing.
He says it's because of the war.

Crouched in the jungle
nothing familiar but fear
death thirsting for victims
he'd figured out how
to separate from his body
watch over himself
from a parallel plane
trusting no one else
with his life.

Not much has changed.
He keeps things from her.
He's usually late
rarely bothers to explain.
She makes allowances.
She'd spent those years
planting a garden
inviting in friends
death not rattling her door.

When she traces scars
jagged and thick
trailing over his shoulder
he flinches
as if she's disturbed
a critical synapse
that keeps him steady.

He comes in her
with such intensity
heat so ferocious
she's afraid
of what it may cost him.

Miami's First POW Home from Korea, 1953

He tries to eat but can't.
It's not that he doesn't want to.
The hum in his head halts him,
marches him further
and further into frostbitten hills,
chains him at dusk in a makeshift cage.
He's lost count of days, nights
prey to artillery of his own men.
Sharp edges pierce a low sky,
release bloody rain
that freezes on contact with the hard soil.

Survival depends on a skinny boy.
You take me with you, the boy says
in halting English, as if it were possible
to simply bow good-bye and head south.
The boy sneaks him clean rice, shoves
a metal cup between bamboo poles.

Now he sits in a diner with the blonde.
He orders a burger and fries, a milk shake.
He wants to be ordinary, do ordinary things.
When the plates arrive, he breaks out in a sweat.
Hands tremble as he tries to pick up the burger.
Aren't you hungry? the girl asks,
dipping fries in a pool of catsup.
He's hungrier than he can remember.
He feels the worm crawl up his anus,
settle in his intestines, waiting
for him to take the first bite,
waiting for its share.

Herman Sharp (1899-1918)

My great uncle was killed at Argonne,
his body buried in foreign soil.
For its first hometown casualty,
Maywood created a park,
inscribed his name in bronze.
Other wars, more dying.
The ground was renamed Veterans Park.
No relative was there to protest
and children who swing on the swings
don't wonder.

Today the only proof I have of his life
is a faded photo postcard.
He's posing in front of a fake cannon,
the Capitol painted as background.
Crisp uniform, broad smile.
His buddy close at his side.
The message: *Dear Mom and Dad,*
See the new watch on my wrist.
How many hours, days until
innocence fell to artillery fire?

Boston's Great Molasses Flood, 1919

On January 15th, it wasn't snow that kept schools closed,
but rivets popping like machine-gun fire, a steel tank bursting,
two million gallons of molten molasses spurting into the air.

First a dark rumble, then a roar, as the North End
turned into a wet, brown hell. Autos and wagons mired,
freight cars crushed, entire buildings crumbled like pasteboard.

The Great War was done; no need to turn molasses
into alcohol for ammunition, but Purity Distilling
demanded one last batch before the end.

Twenty-two dead, horses drowned, hundreds injured.
Clean-up crews and rescuers, knee-deep in makings of rum,
listened as church bells pealed in Prohibition.

Throughout the city, for decades afterwards, they say
you could smell the sweet aroma, and on certain buildings,
if you looked closely, the high water mark left by molasses.

The Bear

Anatoly, a Jewish emigré, tells
a Russian joke in broken English,
over pizza. I nod between mouthfuls
comprehending nothing
except the bear.
When he said he'd left Minsk,
via Canada, to work in the USA,
no endless wait for a visa,
no costly bribes,
I had trouble understanding,
just like I can't follow
the joke about the bear.
A great furry paw whacks
Anatoly's head, sends
his punchline dangling
from a creaky ceiling fan.
Anatoly shakes his fist
at the bear who ruined his joke.
I swear it was
the other way around.

Saving Lives

– for Marvin

You sit in the leather armchair, long past midnight,
working on another scotch, say, *Life is about
housekeeping. Only rarely are we given*

the chance to reach beyond the mundane.
I'm bleary-eyed by now, want you to go home,
hope you won't ask for another refill.

Three children upstairs puckish with sleep,
dream of setting on me, whining about
lost jackets and peanut butter sandwiches.

We know instinctively, you say, *who would risk
their own lives to save a Jew.* We spin out names.
Him, her, not him. Energized, I ask,

How do we decide? I'd seen a man slam his fist,
yell at his kids. *He'll save himself*, I say.
You shake your head.

Lost Boy of Sudan

As soldiers level their rifles to fire,
five-year-old Daniel drops the rope
and slips into the Gilo River.
After miles of dry grass and African sun
how quenching the water will be.
But no friendly river is in this story.
Someone forgot the clock
that belongs in the crocodile's belly,
one ticking so loudly, Daniel must swim
to the other shore for safety.

Here time is shaped by the Baobab,
its root-like branches snarling the sky.
Kick, feral child, while the second-hand
floats free of the vulture's wing.

Lost Boy of Sudan, part 2

In Fargo, some men do the cooking.
Bedroom doors must stay closed.
How strange. For sixteen years Philip
never slept alone. He's terrified of snow
and telephones, wonders why words
don't come out of mouths of people
in photographs. When asked about family,
he keeps silent. How to say parents dead,
brother mauled by lions?
He wants to please, smiles
when they try to explain about hip-hop
and why traffic lights suddenly turn green.

One day he'll return to sun-flooded plains,
herds of long-horned cattle – the bride price.

You Know What I'm Sayin'

– for Balfour

No, I don't know what you're saying, I've been listening to you for over an hour, jiving and feinting, your words slick as the oiled head of a bald man and all I'm getting are whites of your eyes, glassy like you're on something, making you talk like a stamping machine turning out the same die-cast over and over without a brain, or a place to go. You tell me you've been clean and sober for four months–do I look stupid?–four months over the past two years, when you were locked in a ward at Columbia Presbyterian, drying out. Goddamn it, you were the kid at the window–after I'd knocked a dozen times, went away, then knocked again–11 a.m. and you'd just gotten up while the rest of the world was on coffee break and I should have stopped knocking and not looked back but I was a fool and you couldn't stay there with your dad beating you, although not as much anymore because you got bigger and he shrank from all his boozing and coke and trouble with the law, the last time for knifing somebody's wife in a jealous rage and your mother bailed him out like she always did and she won't look at you because you left with me but late at night calls drunk, her tongue lolling on the phone, asking for you, and you out drinking, robbing, screwing white girls because they can afford you and you can't afford them, but you don't listen to the voice in your head, that small part not obliterated by 100 proof gin, not devoured by your father's demons, your mother's anger because you left her to take the beatings and she warns you, don't come looking to borrow the car or mooch a few bucks, that's for the bail bondsman.

No, I don't know what you're saying when you tell me you got a 9 millimeter gun and held up drug dealers in the Bronx, took the A train to Brooklyn to unload the crack–God knows what else–until one of the guys stuck a gun in your face and you

continued

jumped off the subway platform and ran down the tracks to the next stop, two days later checked yourself in for evaluation after you'd tried to OD, which didn't work, and hotel room walls started jerking like a crazy whore, the crack crooning, baby, you and me gonna make sweet music on a bed of thorns and your gut kept hacking at you with razor blades, that's when you wished you had a gun, but you'd loaned it to another motherfucker at the subway station. You tell me this must be hard to take after all I've done for you over the years, you're right, but I don't say anything, because you were a kid with a head full of dreams and a kick-ass swagger, screw the tough love crap, and we'll pretend over supper.

Traveling South by Train through Northern Florida in the 1950's

Swamp gas defines the character of bald cypress, black gum,
tangled Spanish moss suckled by decay, and
flesh-eating plants.
In a clearing the white egret poses in the sun.
Shackled zebra-men pound iron spikes in the opposite track,
securing our return
to the rhythm of wheat fields, morning glory.

The Breaking Yard
Alang, India

After lives spent on the open seas, like dead
whales, they're beached, run aground

as a final resting place. Battered ships and ferries,
hulls rusted, engines past repair, at the mercy of

a thousand men or more, scavenging like rats.
Steel, cables, bells, planking dismantled

with chisels and blow torches; helpless tonnage
winched piece-by-piece and carted off.

The air ripe with stench of rotting cargo,
of men laboring in scorching heat,

lungs seared, skin blackened
from fumes of burning steel and paint.

Men trapped, one misstep from oblivion,
in a listing ship, its prow and stern

unbalanced, crews racing to extract them.
Another bloodied from a falling crane.

For those bone-tired from the constant din,
racked with fevers and parched lips

like seafarers stranded on a mythic shore,
there's cool respite within a ship's bowels,

a world apart from ghost carcasses left
to shimmer in the heat and salty air.

From far-off temples, salvaged bells
ring out, unhindered.

Curacao, 1968
Before the Insurrection

I was there before it happened.
Green lush and pink. Marble floors.
Whisper of cardamon, orange
and hibiscus.
We bought gold and garnets in shops
along the Breedestraat.

Ceiling fans humming, we read
Neruda's poetry, sipped chocolate
from porcelain cups. We drowsed
on sun-dried sheets, made love
to the lilt of Papiamento
rising from servants' quarters.

With our host, the Israeli consul,
we dined on a veranda overlooking
the harbor. Glistening ships.
Waves cradling the pontoon bridge.
No thought to hurry before
the burning.

In the white tiled bathroom,
my hair damp with sea water,
I watched as red ants disappeared
into an invisible crack,
like a rivulet of blood
before the dying.

English Summer
Idmiston, Wiltshire

Warm July evening, roses prickly with thorns,
burbling brook at the rear of the garden.
George, Harry the Horse, and Rusty stop by
the Old Vicarage, our half-timbered rental
– sloping plank floors, brick oven –
for an evening of pontoon, ham sandwiches,
and brew. Down ten quid, George flicks on
the telly for the racing news. Instead
we hear…*one giant leap for mankind.*

Outside, we stare up in silence. The sky,
rife with secrets, has shed another mystery.
We wonder aloud if this could be a hoax.
No matter. An excellent excuse for celebrating
til the 3 a.m. ritual, trucks rattling past the door
on the rutted road from Porton.
Two kilometers away, hidden in the sleepy
countryside, a chemical warfare plant.
Cargo, toxin-filled containers bound for the sea.

118 Maida Vale, London

After shrieking sirens quit,
after dust had settled in the rubble
and the stars resumed their light,
a ragged scar ran three stories
up the north side of the orphaned twin.

Years later, the garden's wild and dun,
saplings choking summer's bloom.
Barbed wire coiled along the fence.
Yet high ceilings set with cherubs
charm us into renting.

The lights blink at weird hours,
floorboards creak and faucets burst.
Steam hisses from dead pipes: perhaps
childish games, high jinks, mischief,
the house lonesome for her mate.

What unruly thing blows up
the dustbin, dangles a dead squirrel
from the eaves or lures the city's
most-wanted thief into our bedroom
in the middle of the night?

Truce, we say, we've months to go.
We've felt your bony fingers.
Today, we'll tidy up the tool shed,
restore the garden's luster
with dahlias, asters, and wild roses.

The Rug Shop

The narrow space brimming with tribal rugs, prayer rugs, silk and wool rugs, hand-dyed, hand-woven, knotted by Afghan women. A stranger, thatch of black hair, black mustache, watching the shop.

A child, about four – *Daddy, look at me* – somersaults, then flops on a striking Balouch. The man flips back rug after rug. I stroke velvet pile, serrated border, stylized leaf, search for the rug I can't resist.

I ask his name – *Amir* – where he's from – *Kabul*. He explains, *I was military pilot for the Taliban* – shrugs – *I had family to feed* – shakes head – *No more. I must fly refugees home* – rubs wrists – *chained up* – shoves hands in pockets – *to be executed*.

On the counter, pamphlets and photos – children torn by shrapnel, shrouded women pelted with rocks, teenager toting a bucket of severed hands, grinning.

Amir lowers his voice as if these rugs have motive. *It wasn't safe. I flee with my family* – child tugs on his leg – *We walk over mountains to Pakistan* – tugs on his hand – *In refugee camp, three years I beg visas* – he scoops up daughter, hugs her.

The shop, an outpost. I first stopped by for war rugs from the Soviet occupation. Only one, a prayer rug, deep red, brown, black, helicopters, tanks, Kalashnikovs woven into a geometric landscape of houses and flowers.

I head toward the door, empty-handed. A large half-priced Hazara sprawls across the front step. I turn to Amir. *Do you miss being a pilot?* He nods – *When I learn better English* – smiles – *I want flying commercial jets for America.*

Annapolis, Maryland
September 6, 2001

The Italian Photo

Hersh was a sergeant, his job reporting casualties,
shells miraculously missing his jeep.
The Germans wanted us to know, he says.
He sits, a loose-limbed old man, at the kitchen table,
crossed legs dangling like a marionette's,
muses over a faded photo
of Mussolini and his mistress swinging
by their heels. Sides of dressed beef.

We mopped up in North Africa, made our way
up the boot to Naples, a filthy city
once you leave the coast, bombardment so loud
we were paralyzed in bunkers.
His long fingers fondle photo edges
as if to quicken his disjointing memory.
At Anzio, you've heard of it, dark-skinned ones
from India went only with knives to slit throats.

Tuscany

The stucco farmhouse roof
is tiled in brilliant orange.
In the yard, colored shirts and sheets
unfurl beneath a cloudy sky.
Chickens peck around an empty washtub
set on hard, swept ground.
Beyond a stone wall, perhaps Etruscan built,
thin silhouettes of stately cypress,
a grove of twisted olive trees.
My father loved this painting.
I was with him in the Village
when he bought it at an outdoor show.

It's not an *important* painting. My father wasn't
a connoisseur of art; he loved things Italian
– opera, fine leather, silk ties,
Mama Leone's eight course dinners.
One day he was going to take the grand tour,
Rome, Florence, Venice,
but he died unexpectedly.

Years later, on a trip to Tuscany,
I drove along the autostrada, turned off
onto narrow winding roads, hoping
beyond the next bend I'd spot the farmhouse.

In Fiesole, I walked along a path
beside a section of the ancient walls,
peered through an opening in the crumbling stones.
Not my father's painted farmyard,
the angle of the roofs was wrong,
but one alive with trailing purple vines,

continued

potted lemon trees, a barking dog.
Leafy plants erupted from a garden plot.
Nearby a white-haired man tended rabbit cages.
For a moment, I was spying on my father.

Cherry Cheesecake

Carl has retinitis pigmentosa,
sight one minute, then
losing it with the shift of his head.
Bright lights to keep
from stumbling into corners.
He's not ready to give up
what belongs to the eye.

I hesitate to say, *Just make an X*,
place my finger where I want him
to sign his name.
With heavy black marker
in his right hand,
he slowly forms letters,
his left forefinger, a guide.

The next time, he shows me
a new voice-activated cell phone
and offers me cherry cheesecake.
I'm learning to cook as a blind man,
he says. *Easier than fighting it.*
Cherries are sliding off the top
of a pinkish, lopsided slice.

I close my eyes,
feel my way with a fork.

Lark Sparrow

Cissie, 88, fragile white feather,
fingers the filigree lace on her gown,
removes the oxygen tube from her nose,
and says for 37 years
she scrubbed the same kitchen floor
on her hands and knees.

> *I remember Queen Anne's lace and thistles*
> *wild on the prairie but violets preferred*
> *the creek bank's damp earth.*

She has no children but a grandniece
begs her to return to England.
Pressing a light paisley shawl
to the side of her head,
"There are drafts," Cissie says.

> *At the sound of thunder, cotton-tails*
> *and golden pheasants scurried for cover.*

She points to a hand-tinted photo
of a thickset man, his nose
grotesquely flattened.
"My husband was so handsome
until someone nearly killed him."

> *The horizon reached out*
> *to old Indian burial grounds, bulldozers*
> *standing by for a generation.*

A large bluish vein cradles her face.
"As much as I want to go home,"
Cissie says, "I would never leave
Sam buried here by himself."

> *I remember the lark sparrow's trill,*
> *bluestem shuddering up its seed*
> *when wind swept over the prairie.*

About the Author

Nancy Scott was born in Illinois and graduated from the University of Chicago in 1960. Her social activism began in college when she volunteered as a Girl Scout troop leader on Chicago's South Side. Now living in New Jersey, she has spent decades as an advocate for foster and adoptive children, abused children, the homeless and the mentally ill. In 1996, as an outlet for the myriad of stories she'd heard in her work on the streets, she started writing poetry. Current managing editor of *U.S.1 Worksheets*, she is a recipient of a Ragdale Residency and her poetry and short fiction have appeared in many literary journals.

www.ingramcontent.com/pod-product-compliance
Lightning Source LLC
Chambersburg PA
CBHW071009080526
44587CB00015B/2405